THAT'S NOT MY ENDING!

Written by Sharon Morrissey

Illustrated by Romina Petra

THAT'S NOT MY ENDING!

Written by Sharon Morrissey
Illustrated by Romina Petra

Second Edition

ISBN: 9798714914010

Independently published by Sharon Morrissey.

KIND WORDS FOR
THAT'S NOT MY ENDING!

Parents: read this book—first for yourself and then for your children. You will be glad you did.

Divorce is tough on everyone. And, everyone needs comfort and support. This book does that, and more.

The story of Seanie and Toni is true—this is what happens to children and to their parents. Their story is a comforting and helpful tale of how parents and children can find their way through scary and uncertain times.

Children can get lost in the upheaval of their parents' divorce. They retreat into their own worlds. They have no control over their parents' decisions; they just have to live with them. So they look for ways to cope with uncertainty and unpredictability. Some may not be able to tell their parents what they need. Others assume their parents are too busy, too angry, too distracted, or too worried.

But, there is a way through these difficult times. This beautifully written and illustrated book gives both parents and children a way to come together, to talk honestly about how divorce is upending their lives. And, by talking, it's possible to find good, practical solutions.

Please read and use this book!

Michael D. Lang, Mediator, Trainer, Consultant and Coach

TABLE OF CONTENTS

PERSONAL REASONS FOR WRITING THIS BOOK, AND WHAT I AM LEARNING.

This book is for all of us who continue to write our endings.

I have worked with children for more than half of my life. I specialise in working with children and adults who have come from separated families. I practice Humanistic Family Mediation. My family is a separated family. It is what we call a "blended family," meaning it's a lot of different types of families together.

I have two stepsons, a daughter (I am divorced from her dad), a daughter (I am married to her dad), and we fostered a little person. We truly are a blended family.

Important to know for those of us in blended families

DO WE LIKE EACH OTHER? Most of the time.

DO WE FIGHT? Absolutely.

DO WE LOVE EACH OTHER? Most of the time.

When we all "got married" for the second time, I believed it would be great. I read books telling me, that everyone would "blend" into a new way of working within a family system and of course, it had moments when it was great and moments when it was very difficult. It was, and continues to be very hard at times. We are all older, and we have learned what we will and will not accept from each other, but we had to sit down and talk it out. It took a lot of courage, honesty and vulnerability to be able to do that.

I read books to my children about having two homes, with parents who loved them but couldn't love each other. Did that work? I'm unsure if it did. I wonder if framing relationship breakdowns the way we do, scares us and our children even more?

What we need to be able to do as adults is listen. Did I listen? Not all the time. It was hard to be emotionally present when I was going through my relationship breakdown. It, was also difficult to be physically present as I was working. We need to balance our hurts, with the hurt of our children.

So, from personal and professional experience, this book was born.

WHO IS THIS BOOK FOR?

This book is for our children who are with us on the journey of relationship breakdown. I believe it gives them (and us as parents) a realistic expectation of the separation process.

Relationships with parents, siblings, grandparents, family and friends will be strained, angry, sad and dislocated. It also looks at the fact that this relationship breakdown is not the fault of the child. This book takes blame away.

This book is for those of us, children and parents, who continue to re-write our endings. We continue to be a work in progress.

Initially, it would be my advice that parents read this book on their own, and look at the "NOTE FOR PARENTS" section at the back to pre-empt possible questions children will have. Take time to think about meaningful and appropriately honest answers.

It is our role as parents to steady the ship when the seas are choppy. When as the parent, you have taken time to read and to digest the information, you may become aware of little signs to note and be mindful of.

I am hoping this book will form a suite of books for children and for parents. We need to know there isn't always a "happy ever after," and the two homes may not be warm and cosy but tinged with sadness, fear, loss and anger.

IMPORTANT NOTE FOR PARENTS AND GUARDIANS:

If you are reading this book, I imagine you are in the process, or beginning the process of relationship breakdown. This is not an easy road, and I urge you to look after yourselves during this time.

As adults, we find navigating the loss of our relationship devastating, and at times, it is difficult to see beyond our own pain. As parents, we need to. We need to make sure we are available to our children.

This book is a look at parental separation through the eyes of Seanie (10) and his sister Toni (9), and the impact it has on them. Seanie and Toni could be any one of our children, so in an attempt to see how they feel, we will travel the journey with them.

SHARON MORRISSEY
Mediation and Conflict Resolution
"solutions as individual as you"

www.sharonmorrisseyconflictresolution.ie
sharonmorrisseymediation@gmail.com
+353 87 695 9346

NOTE FOR CHILDREN:

Hello everybody,

My name is Sharon, and I have written this book for you and the people who love and care for you, with the help of children just like you.

If you are reading this book, your family must be in the middle of a huge change. It is hard to feel ok in these times; perhaps you feel angry sad, relieved, and a little shaky.

I have worked with children in your situation for a long time. What I have learned from speaking with children is that if we talk it out and are honest with one another, all these changes are a little less scary. What is most important is to know that your family is not ending; it is changing, sometimes whether we want it to or not. Change can be frightening, but change can also be good.

All these feelings are NORMAL. Your feelings are normal, and you are a normal person, having a normal response to a difficult situation.

THIS IS NOT YOUR FAULT!

Here is the story of two children whom I have met along the way (I have made up their names), and in these children, there is a bit of how we all feel when our family changes. Remember it is changing, not ending.

All these events are based on years of working alongside children. When we hurt, we start to become aware of how and where the pain is stuck inside of us. Sometimes this pain can make us really sick. Sometimes, the sick feeling is in our body, like tummy aches and headaches; sometimes, it is in our heart and mind, for example, being really angry, sad or unhappy. Sometimes, we let it out by boxing someone or something, and other times, we are so sad, we stop talking, and that hurts us on the inside.

We live with our Mom and Dad in a beautiful big house. It has a big garden and a pond, and we have two fish: GOLDI and FOXI. Seanie loves playing football.

GOLDI AND FOXI swim around and around in their pond. They look happy. We love to watch how they blow bubbles when they talk. We wonder what they talk about?

14

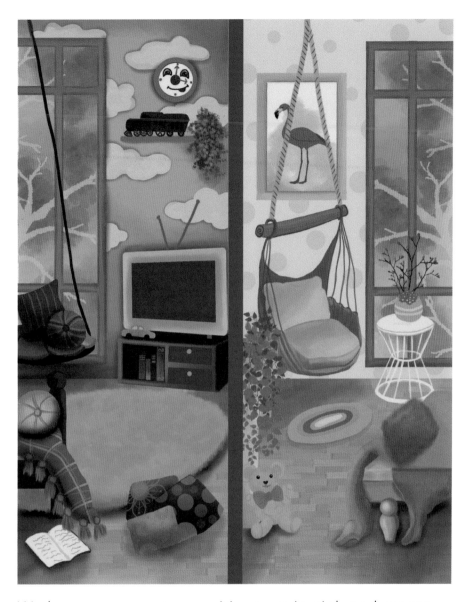

We have our own rooms. My room is pink and cream; Seanie's room is cream and blue. We have books and toys, and Seanie has a TV. I don't have a tele but that's ok. I spend a lot of time in Seanie's room.

We were happy and had fun before, but now Mom and Dad argue.

THEY SHOUT AND ARGUE A LOT.

I think about my fish talking to each other. I wonder do they hear Mom and Dad shouting outside?

Seanie says he doesn't care about the shouting. I think he cares. Sometimes, I see his eyes and they look wet. His tears never fall.

We don't tell Mom and Dad. They seem sad also, and we are sure their bellies hurt too.

They don't look at us or at each other. Our big house seems small and grey with nowhere to go.

One evening, Mom and Dad ask us to sit down in the sitting room. They tell us they love us, but they don't love each other. They tell us they are splitting up, separating, and this **SEPARATION** is not our fault. They tell us that Dad is moving out, and he has a flat in town. We don't want Dad to go.

"What's a flat?" I ask. "What's **SEPARATING?**"
"Isn't a flat a piece of furniture?"

Dad explains that a flat is a "house" in a building with other houses. We think it sounds exciting. Dad says we can stay with him and see him all the time. I don't know what that means; we see him all the time now. I feel confused. Seanie is quiet and asks to go to his room. I follow. I still do not know what "**SEPARATED**" means.

THE DOOR CLOSES AND WE HEAR MOM CRYING.

I don't like when Seanie goes red because I know he is cross and sad. I leave to find Mom to ask her what separation is. Mom is sitting in the kitchen crying. Dad is not in the house. Mom says she has a book for us, it's about **DIVORCING** parents. I don't know what separating and divorce is. Mom reads the book to me it says we will all end up being friends in the end.

SEPARATING the book says is when grown up people who may (or may not) have children break up the relationship they have with each other

BUT THE BOOK SAYS WE WILL ALL BE FRIENDS IN THE END.

Daddy moved out to his flat. We go to see him every week. It is not like the flat in the divorce book. Dad's flat is small and dark on the inside, and the stairwell doesn't smell nice. Seanie and Daddy sleep in one room. Daddy's room has a big bed. Daddy leaves the door of the bedroom open and I sleep on the couch. It's a bit lumpy, and I don't like the shadows on the wall. The flat has no room for a fishpond. It is always noisy at Dad's flat.

When Daddy comes to collect us, this is called "**ACCESS.**" We have access to our Dad. Mom seems sad or angry and gives out a lot, and Dad gives out a lot too. We tell them to stop giving out, but they don't. They shout that this is "adult stuff," but it's not; they are shouting at each other about us.

Mom gives out when we go to Dads flat, and she gives out when we come back. Dad does the same. They give out at us and at each other. Their faces get red and angry. We hear them talk and shout on the phone about court.

A **COURT** is where a **JUDGE** who is a very important woman or man tells Mom and Dad what they have to do to look after us. I ask Seanie about court. He says court is a place where people go when they do bad things and when they fight. Seanie says they are fighting over us. Why are Mom and Dad fighting over us?

Seanie is cross all the time now. I don't go into his room to watch tele anymore, so I talk to my fish, Foxi and Goldi. I still like looking at their bubbles. I imagine they are telling me that it will be ok, but I don't know what "ok" means. I don't like school. I don't have friends, and everything seems sad and grey. Sometimes, I can see the teacher talking, but I cannot hear what she says. Sometimes, I see children whispering behind their hands or pointing at me.

THIS MAKES ME MAD OR SAD.

Seanie and I hear about court, access, **MAINTENANCE** and who does
what. We hear about money and two houses and who loves us more.
We want to believe Mom and Dad love us the same. This is what they
always say. It makes us scared when we remember them saying they
don't love each other anymore; maybe they don't love us now?

28

Seanie says grownups are "stupid." Seanie is very cross all the time. I feel lonely. I miss my Mom and Dad and Seanie too. He says **MAINTENANCE** is about money.

I still have Foxi and Goldi, and we talk all the time, and they blow their bubbles back to me.

RIGHT NOW, NOBODY IS HAPPY. WE HAVE FORGOTTEN "HAPPY".

The book Mom gave me says we will be friends in the end. There are no friends in this big, grey house or in this small, dark flat.

Everything was good...until that "talk" in the sitting room. We can't remember much of that talk. We think Dad left because we fight and argue. We fight and argue all the time now.

Now, we feel black. Everything is dark. Neither of us want people to talk to us. We don't want people to look at us. We see them whispering in class and in the yard. We know it's us they are talking about. Seanie says he wants to punch people and has to try very hard not to. It's all getting harder.

Weekly Planner

Monday
Tuesday
Wednesday
Thursday
Friday
Saturday
Sunday

We really don't like Wednesday evenings. Dad collects us from school, and we see our friends whispering. We don't want to get in the old blue car and go to the flat. The flat is awful. It's dark and at the top of a very long, smelly stairs.

Most of all, Seanie hates missing football practice. He loves football, and is very good at it. He can't do football anymore because we go to Dad's on Wednesdays.

It was supposed to be happy being at Dad's, but no one asked us when we would like to go. Now Seanie says he is not good at anything, not football, or being a brother. I tell him he is a great brother.

THEY SAID THEY WOULD ASK US.

They never asked us what we wanted. Not once.

We were told what to do. We weren't asked. It makes us so angry.

Court says we are to go to Dads on Wednesdays (football day) and every second weekend, so Seanie misses football practice, and I miss my fish. We both miss Mom and worry about her when we are not there. We miss Dad when we are with Mom. We always feel tired, but when we go to bed, our head races and it's very hard to sleep

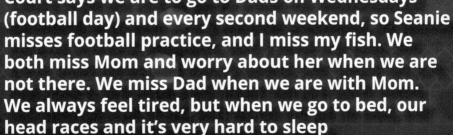

We get bothered when we hear Mom crying or shouting at us. We wonder what is wrong with her? Those books she gave us said we would figure it out and we would all be friends. We are not figuring it out, and we are not friends. It feels as if we don't like each other.

We are glad that we have each other. Even
though we fight, we can talk to each other.
We know our insides are hurting.

Mom is pale all the time. Her skin is white and her eyes are dark. She is so skinny, so when we hug her, we are afraid she will break. Mom used to laugh a lot, but now she doesn't laugh or smile; her heart is sad.

When we go home to Mom after school, we always know if she has been crying. It is hard to describe. We never see her crying; we just know. It is a feeling.

Mom gets angry a lot. She shouts about "that man" and she tells us to "tell your father." This makes us so prickly. He is our Dad, not "that man." We don't like it when Mom says, "Tell your father I need money for dancing or swimming."

When we tell "that man" (Dad) that Mom says we need money for dancing or swimming, Dad gets cross and says, "SHE (Mom) should go get a job!" And his face blows up like a balloon and goes all red. Seanie and I look at each other. We know that this is not the time to say that Mom has a job. It's the one she's always had at her office, and we really don't get to see her very much at all.

Dad's face is all red now, and his shirts are bigger. Seanie and I think it's because the kitchen in the flat is old and the takeaway is at the bottom of the stairwell. It's really cool for a treat, but we think Daddy is treating himself every night.

When Seanie and I talk about this, we wonder what it is going to be like for our birthday celebrations and Aunty Lena's wedding next year. We are so worried about how it will be if "SHE" and "THAT MAN"—our Mom and Dad—are there together, or will they be there together? We wonder if they have forgotten that they are our Mom and Dad?

How will we get Mom and Dad to hear what we are worried and frightened about? How do we tell them they need to listen to us? How can we tell them that we are angry, sad and frightened?

They said it was not our fault, but Mom and Dad used to live together in our smiling house, but now they cannot stand to look at each other.

We have questions for Mom and Dad. There are things Seanie and I want to ask them. Why do we have to split our time. We want to ask them, but we are too afraid that they will get cross or cry, so we have decided to write them down. We are going to leave the questions on the table in the house for Mom and the other questions for Dad in his flat, so they will know the postman didn't bring it.

- What did we do to make you stop liking each other?

- Was it because we were fighting and we wouldn't share? What if we promise we will never fight again? Will you live together then?

- Why do I have to miss football and go to Dad's house? Why can't Dad come to our house?

- Why do you call each other "she" and "that man" or "YOUR MOTHER" and "YOUR FATHER?"

- Why do we have to split our time between two houses?

- What will happen on our birthdays and at Christmas? What will happen to our Mom or Dad if we are not there? Who will give Mom/Dad Christmas dinner?

We know that Mom and Dad are cross and sad. Mom cries and Dad shouts, but we are cross and sad and angry too. We miss our things when we are at the other house. We miss our beds and our rooms. We miss our old world. It's not like it was before; our hearts feels heavy and black, and we are not sure if it will ever get better.

WE CAN'T BE HAPPY IF OUR MOM AND DAD ARE SAD.

How can we be happy opening gifts if Dad is sitting on his own in that dark flat, or if Mom is here in the sitting room when we are at Dad's?

How do we fix this? What should we do? How do we make it so we can tell you?

On a Thursday afternoon, after getting in trouble at school, we sat at the kitchen table and started to cry.

It all came out—all the grey and all the sad. We did it together.

We told Mom about how sad we were and about how it was not like in the book they showed us on the"talk" day. We explained that the people in our family are not friends, and it doesn't look like it will be ok.

Seanie explained that we are scared about birthdays, Christmas, and about how he hated missing football. I kept crying.

MOM LISTENED AND SHE CRIED TOO.

Mom said she was so sorry she had not listened to us. Mom said she would speak with Dad through an email tonight. Mom and Dad decided to go visit someone who will help them talk to each other about us. They went to see a **MEDIATOR**. A mediator is a person who helps families talk and listen to each other without arguing, and then make new decisions. The mediator helped Mom and Dad and now they text each other about playdates for the weekends.

We now have a plan. On Thursday evenings, Seanie, Mom and I sit and tell each other how the week has been.

Mom says she will text Dad about the football training, matches, birthday parties and playdates for the weekends when we are at Dad's. We don't

know what that is, but we think it might work, because Mom calls Dad "Dad" now, and Dad calls Mom "Mom."

We also talk to Dad on Friday and tell him how the week has been. When we don't go to Dad's on the weekend, we ring him for a chat and to tell him how the spelling test went. Dad helps with our homework on Wednesdays. When we go with Dad on Friday, we use Dad's phone to call Mom and tell her how the spelling test went. We are learning to talk to each other again.

For now, we have decided that this is our ending....

"**WHEN WE GET ANGRY,
WHEN WE FIGHT,
WE HAVE PROMISED THAT WE WILL WRITE,
WRITE IT DOWN AND GET IT OUT,
SO THERE IS NO NEED TO SHOUT.**"

And so it is. We are working on our ending as a new beginning....

ACKNOWLEDGEMENTS:

To my husband, Moss: you believe in me always; thank you and I love you. To my girls, Molly, Lizzy and Belle, and boys, Kevin and Eoin, thank you.

I wish to acknowledge the learning from the experience of life.

I continue to learn. I am grateful to have met the people I have who have provided learning opportunities.

Thank you to the person who helped me realise my path was different and who taught me to be aware that all may not be what it seems.

ABOUT THE AUTHOR:

Sharon Morrissey is one of Ireland's leading experts and training consultants in Mediation and Conflict Resolution. Sharon's role in Family Mediation provides a dignified and humane way of resolving disputes, helping parties to reach an agreement that is workable and sustainable. Sharon is determined to support parents to consciously co-parent during parental and family breakdown. She practices Humanistic Family Mediation.

Sharon has witnessed the devastating effects of relationship breakdown on individuals, families and especially children.

This book aims to support children ages 7-10 (approximately) whose parents are going through separation and divorce. It also aims to support parents to support their children.

Sharon has lectured in Conflict Coaching and Family Mediation at St. Angela's College Sligo Ireland and in the Law Society in Ireland. She lectures in Family Mediation, Understanding Conflict, Mediation Theory and Practice and Reflective Practice.

She has worked in the community and voluntary sector for over 25+ years, and during this time, she has sat on Boards of Management and Childcare Committees, always advocating for the Voice of the Child.

Sharon is also pursuing further research on Self-Reflection by practitioners in Family Mediation and on how this ensures families are receiving the best service possible for them.

Sharon can be contacted via her website
(WWW.SHARONMORRISSEYCONFLICTRESOLUTION.IE),
on Facebook (Sharon Morrissey Family Mediation/Family Support Service), LinkedIn and Instagram.

ABOUT THE ILLUSTRATOR.

 Hello,

My name is Romina and I was born in Romania in 1989.

Both of my parents are artists in their own right- and instilled a love of all things creative from an early age.

Currently, I am living in Germany with my life partner.

I settled in Germany after widespread travel throughout Europe when I completed my studies of Graphic Arts in college.

I am also a passionate photographer.

Approximately five years ago a friend of mine introduced me to the concept of illustrating children's books. From that point onwards, I have made connections around the world, illustrating for many amazing authors.

While working with individual authors, I learn more and this motivates me to continue to upgrade and improve my skills.

I believe that everything happens for a reason and I am so thankful to be a part if this creative journey.

Email: Rominapetrablaga@gmail.com

FURTHER KIND WORDS.

That's Not My Ending! is quite an inside-out story by Sharon Morrissey. Her artistry applied from personal and professional experience weaves provocative themes, seeking to give children the words and permission to experience and share their own stories. I think she succeeds. I succumbed to the temptation of expropriating the title for use as my mantra. But where I had to struggle decades to experience my loss in order to share it and heal, That's Not My Ending! offers children and parents an opportunity to get right down to business. Which is to say, when I was Seanie's age, it was not my ending either. I especially like the exclamation point.

In addition to the load taken on by Toni and Seanie, the story conveys the regression of the parents and their inability to stay present as loving adults for the children as a result of their own trauma, which is something many of us can identify with. This got me thinking of each parent as the goose who lays the golden egg and how important it is for each to somehow find affirmation, guidance and perspective in healthy triangulation, i.e., healthy intimates, therapy and mediation to get what they need to be present for their children. And of course, none of us gainfully do life alone, even under the best of circumstances. It did seem a stretch to imagine the children coming up with those bottom-line questions to pose to their parents, but they serve a purpose and seem within the realm of possibility, especially when they find life as they know it on the line.

Overall, the book seems to hit the issues that a 7- to 10-year-old going through the losses of divorce could relate to. And what a heads-up for parental collaboration in the service of their children's welfare. Thanks for sharing.

Dan Murphy, Childcare Centre Manager

This book conveys a fundamentally important message to separating families and their children: it is OK not to be OK in the wake of relationship breakdown, and it is important to keep talking to each other. Using easily understandable and appropriate language, Sharon conveys the heartbreak and confusion children may feel, and she gives practical, concrete advice while avoiding the platitudes that so often feature in literature on relationship breakdown.

A must for any separating parent and their children.

Sabine Walsh, Mediator, Trainer, and Lecturer

For couples experiencing conflict in relationship breakdown, this book provides extremely useful insight into the child's perspective and experience. It is a valuable reminder not just of the importance of allowing children to be heard, but also the importance of really listening, and this includes listening not just with your ears, but with your eyes. Through the individual eyes of Toni and Seanie, Sharon also highlights the effect separation can have on the sibling relationship—a fact that is very often overlooked. Most importantly, it's a message of hope for those struggling with relationship breakdown. You can change your ending!

Deirdre Burke, Solicitor at Burke Legal, The Abbey Centre, St. Patricks Road, Wicklow

THAT'S NOT MY ENDING! FOR PARENTS

Dear Parents,

For this book to be as supportive as possible to you and your children, there are some things I have learned from my training and from working with children and families in similar situations to yours over the last twenty (or more) years. I will attempt to guide you through the book with the main learnings from Seanie and Toni, and what their behaviour is attempting to communicate. By doing this, I am hoping it may prepare you as the parent for some of the questions and concerns your children may have.

As parents, we try to shield our children from the conflict within relationship breakdown; however, children see, hear and most importantly KNOW us better than we know ourselves. At one point, their very survival depended on us as parents and parent people, so children have learned what they need to do to be part of the family system.

Children will feel when parents are sad, happy, angry, etc., even if we tell them we are "fine." Attachment studies with babies and their primary caregiver have proven this scientifically. By not speaking about the issues with our children, we are inadvertently teaching them to deny their feelings. As parents in a relationship breakdown situation, we do not do this on purpose.

On the other hand, it is very important to be aware of overburdening our children with adult content. It is a balancing act. However, you both are parents to your children and therefore have an intimate knowledge of how to honestly and appropriately speak to them. Children function better when there is an acknowledgement and an honesty about their situation that is age- and stage-appropriate. In conflictual relationship situations, we see siblings attempting to protect each other. Each sibling will bring a different skill set to the relationship of protection within the familial breakdown, and none of the children will experience the relationship breakdown the same. This makes looking after each child (plus yourself) a daunting task. It will also depend on a number of factors before the relationship broke down, such as the following:

- Was there a good communication routine in the house?
- How did children interact with other siblings and with each parent?
- Were you aware that each sibling had a different type of relationship with you and your partner?

Whereas the different relationships may have been accepted before, in a relationship breakdown, these relationships and specifically the differences may become contentious. It is imperative that relationships are not undermined or used in a negative way between siblings and parents.

When children are aware of the conflict and have to deal with it on their own—by this, I mean it has not been overtly addressed—it affects all areas of their lives. Children will find it hard to sleep, and if they do sleep, it may not be restful. The emotional and physical tiredness impacts children's ability to learn and maintain relationships in school. It affects their ability to speak directly with their parents. Children do not want to be an additional burden on what they feel is a traumatic situation. There is a sense of wanting to disappear, feeling grey, and having nowhere to go/hide. The secure base, whatever or whomever that may be, is changing. The familiar is unfamiliar.

Seanie and Toni's parents tell the children they "love them, but they don't love each other." From my experience of talking with children in this situation, the major concern for children is, what happens if Mom and Dad stop loving us? Will we have to go too?

As parents, is it possible that you both can speak to your children together? Can you agree in advance on what you are going to say to your children and how it will be phrased?

Try and avoid "fluffy" explanations, but equally avoid blaming explanations. Remember, the children you created as a couple, you created equally. They are 50% Mom and 50% Dad. By blaming or disrespecting the other parent, the children will internalise these feelings and take that negativity on board. For stepchildren, foster children and adopted children, the impact is equally devastating. As a couple, you created a family unit, and the positive relationships you worked hard for need to be preserved.

Children will initially think of the idea of two homes as exciting, and this again can cause hurt to the resident parent. Again, practically and from my experience, the left parent feels abandoned and the excitement of the children going to the non-resident parent can cause huge conflict between the parents and the children.

During relationship breakdown, we see loss for the children emerging. Sibling relationships become strained as each sibling tries to process the potential outcomes alone. It is important that children have support during this time. The support may come naturally from grandparents, extended family, close friends, clubs and extra-curricular activities. Parents need to be mindful of the child who appears to be managing well and wondering why that is and who is offering support. Sometimes, children will need more structured support, for example, counselling and play therapy.

Parents need to be watchful of the quantity of changes in the children's lives. These include the following:
- Separation of parents
- Possible change of house
- Schools
- Friends, etc.
- Change of routine and contact
- Children may be embarrassed about the separation

When children do not want to go on contact visits, it may not be that they do not want to see the other parent; it may have to do with the change of routine. We know that children need routine to feel safe and secure. Can you include your children's plans in access?

Within Seanie and Toni's house during this time, we see a deterioration in the relationship they have with each other. This could be the result of a variety of factors, e.g., separation and a change in homes, routines, and schedules, but also a change of roles. During times of change within the family, the original roles assigned may be changed, causing further upset within the family system. In this case, it might be that Seanie directly or indirectly has taken the new role of "man of the house" and has changed his role as far as Toni is concerned.

Seanie may now be attempting to discipline and direct Toni, instead of his previous role as big brother.

Inevitably, children blame themselves. They make the breakdown of the relationship their fault in their own minds, and they try to "fix" it. "We didn't do our chores, we didn't do well in school, we were always fighting," etc. Children believe they can control the outcome by "being good," and when this happens, their parents will get back together. It is fundamental that children are reassured around this. When children feel they have no control, they inherit behaviours that will give them control in some area of their life. These behaviours can be positive or negative, e.g., exceling in school, sports, music, etc. or bullying and aggressive behaviours, self-harming and eating disorders. If possible, parents should have open and honest communication with their child's school so the child is being supported all the time.

During the process of separation, children's feelings and emotions, as well as the parents, are in turmoil.

As a guide for families, I use the stages of grief as a template. The loss of a significant relationship is, after all, a loss.

These stages are
  • Denial and shock
  • Pain and guilt
  • Anger and bargaining
  • Depression/reflection/loneliness
  • Acceptance and reconstruction

These feelings swing like a pendulum for parents and children, and they realistically will come and go throughout life. The positive outcome we can hope for is that we as parents have self-awareness about the movability of the feelings so we can be present to support our children with these stages as needed.

Children will worry. They will worry equally about each parent, and they will be angry with both parents, sometimes one more than the other, but the feelings and concerns will continue.

For parents, it is important to refer to ex-spouse as Mom/Dad, or by their names. It is essential to be soft in the tone we use. It is vital to convey, in so far as possible, a positive regard for the person who is your co-parent. Do not allow your current (possibly justified) negative view of the other parent to depreciate their relationship with their children.

CHILD PROTECTION

The premise for everything here is that children are of paramount importance and their needs and rights are respected. Children have the right to be safe. Child protection is an obligation.

It is also imperative to be aware of the things you did not like within your ex-spouse's parenting style but put up with because you were married. These areas will still exist after the relationship breakdown. How are these areas going to be managed now?

This book is meant to support you as you support your children during this vulnerable time.

Parents will be parents forever; parents will also one day possibly become grandparents. There will be school and college graduations, religious celebrations, birthdays, weddings, christenings and funerals where you will need to hold a space for your children to be. This involves sharing the space with your ex-partner.

The best way to do this is to establish a new and more formal way of communicating. This can be achieved officially by employing a mediator, or through a court process, or informally by speaking directly to each other, if this is possible. Do not use your children to carry messages from one parent to the other.

I offer mediation services to parties to set up formal ways of communication. I also offer child-focussed and child-inclusive mediations. To support children, I offer practical family support, giving children a space to speak about areas that are concerning them.

For further information, please visit my website
WWW.SHARONMORRISSEYCONFLICTRESOLUTION.IE

I wish you the very best on this journey.

Printed in Great Britain
by Amazon